Accelerated Wealth:
Using Velocity and Offset
Banking to Break Free from Debt

B.F. Weaver

Copyright © 2012 B.F. Weaver

All rights reserved.

ISBN: 9798303555907

To my amazing wife and two beautiful daughters,

This book is for you — the reason I push forward every day. Every step I take is with the goal of securing the future we deserve and the financial freedom we've always dreamed of. Your love, patience, and belief in me inspire everything I do. I am so grateful for you and all that we will achieve together.

With all my love,

-B.

CONTENTS

	Acknowledgments	i
1	My Journey to Financial Freedom	1
2	Understanding Velocity Banking and the Power of a Personal Line of Credit (PLOC)	11
3	Consolidation and Elimination of Debt	17
4	Gaining Assets through Velocity Banking	24
5	Home Equity Line of Credit (HELOC)	31
6	Putting It All Together	62
7	Step-By-Step Guide to Using Velocity and Offset Banking Together	69

ACKNOWLEDGMENTS

First and foremost, I want to express my deepest gratitude to my amazing wife and two beautiful daughters. Your love, patience, and unwavering support have been the foundation of this journey. Every step I take is inspired by the life we are building together, and this book is a testament to your belief in me.

A special thank you to J.J., whose guidance and mentorship opened my eyes to the true power of financial independence. Your wisdom has shown me how achieving financial freedom is not only a gift to myself but to my entire family. I am forever grateful for your insight and encouragement.

With gratitude,

-B

MY JOURNEY TO FINANCIAL FREEDOM

A Life of Financial Struggles

Growing up, my family worked hard to ensure we had the essentials. We were never hungry, always had a roof over our heads, and somehow managed to make ends meet. But beyond the basics—food, shelter, school supplies—comfort was a foreign concept. New clothes, the latest gadgets, or the luxuries you see in commercials? Those were beyond our reach. I'll never forget the way I felt walking into my friends' houses, where everything seemed so perfect—their new cars, the fresh clothes, the latest video games—while we were scrimping just to keep the lights on. But honestly, I never felt deprived. We understood our limits and made do with what we had. My parents always made sure we knew that love and family were the most important things, not possessions or the latest trends.

What I did feel, though, was the constant weight of financial stress. My mom worked herself to the bone just to keep us afloat. She was always stretching every dollar, often sacrificing her own needs to make sure we didn't go without. I remember her telling me stories about how she would skip meals so we could have extra food or how she would find ways to mend our clothes to make them last longer. Despite her best efforts, there was never enough to feel truly secure. I never saw her relax, always calculating the next move, juggling bills, and trying to make the paycheck stretch.

Looking back, I can see how that uncertainty shaped me. We were trapped in a system that didn't seem designed to help people like us get ahead. Growing up in Northern California didn't make things easier—high cost of living, expensive housing, and natural disasters that always seemed to hit when we were least prepared. I still remember the fire that wiped out our home, leaving us with nothing but the clothes on our backs. That experience taught me two things: life can change in an instant, and no matter how hard you work, it sometimes feels like the system is stacked against you.

But despite all the struggles, my parents gave me something invaluable: a relentless work ethic. They instilled in me the belief that if you work hard enough, you can make it. Sports were where I learned to push myself, and I know now that the lessons from those days shaped every decision I've made since. But here's the question that haunts me now: What if I had learned the basics of financial freedom back then? Where might I be today?

As a kid, I dreamed of having the things I couldn't afford—those shiny new sneakers, the toys everyone else seemed to have. But as I grew older, my priorities shifted. If I ever had kids, I promised myself they wouldn't face the same struggles. I wouldn't just buy them things; I wanted to give them experiences—memories that would last a lifetime. Because in the end, memories mean more than stuff. **It's those moments that create the bonds, the**

laughter, and the stories that define our lives—not the new toys or gadgets that fade away.

A Wake-Up Call

By the time I hit 28, I had already experienced a few wake-up calls. I was coasting along, trying to figure out life, but it wasn't until I took a hard look at my finances that I realized just how little I knew. Growing up, there was no conversation about how money really worked—just the bare minimum of paying bills and hoping to stay afloat. My parents did the best they could, but there was never any guidance on how to build wealth or create financial independence. I didn't understand credit, savings, investing, or any of the critical tools that could help me thrive.

I moved to Sacramento for college—becoming the first in my family to go—and let me tell you, it was one hell of a ride. I shared a cramped two-bedroom apartment with three friends while we attended a local junior college. After paying rent, I barely had enough for food or gas. I made it work with whatever I could scrounge up—hunting trips, Velveeta mac and cheese, and ramen. It wasn't glamorous, but it was survival. The worst part? I thought this was just normal, that everyone was struggling in the same way, so I never questioned it.

After three semesters, I dropped out. I was burned out, directionless, and honestly, I felt like a failure. But now, looking back, I see that was one of the best decisions I ever made. It forced me to find another way. I didn't just want to survive anymore; I wanted to understand life on a deeper level. I knew education was important, but I also knew that learning from the school of hard knocks could be just as valuable. So, I took whatever jobs I could—first at a Harley Davidson shop, then at a restaurant—just to pay the bills.

But deep down, I knew this wasn't a sustainable way of living. There had to be more to life than just scraping by.

Then I made a life-changing decision: I enlisted in the military. And let me tell you—it was one of the best decisions of my life. Not only did it give me a steady paycheck, but it opened up a world of opportunities I never could have imagined. I traveled the world, saw places I'd only dreamed about, and, most importantly, I met my wife—my partner in this journey. Together, we built a family, and our two beautiful daughters became my driving force. They were my purpose.

But even with all the perks of military life, my finances were still a mess. I was living paycheck to paycheck, making the classic mistakes—overspending, racking up debt, and failing to save for the future. It wasn't until about seven years into my military career that I had a wake-up call. I realized I was seriously behind in financial literacy. I had to make a change. That's when I decided to change my life. I began reading books, listening to podcasts, and seeking out mentors who could help me understand how money truly worked. My financial education began, and I became hungry for knowledge. The more I learned, the more I realized that building wealth wasn't about luck—it was about strategy.

Absolutely! Here's the expanded version of each section, with additional details to give each one depth, providing a clearer picture of your financial journey and the key milestones that led to your success.

My Current Status and What I've Achieved

Looking back, I'm honestly shocked at how far I've come. There was a time when I felt like I was stuck in quicksand, with no way to escape the overwhelming stress of debt, living paycheck to paycheck, constantly worrying about how

I would make ends meet. But that's no longer my reality. It didn't happen overnight, but through dedication, perseverance, and learning from my mistakes, I've transformed my life and my financial situation in ways I couldn't have imagined. The difference is night and day. I no longer feel trapped. Instead, I feel in control.

The control I've gained over my finances has given me a sense of freedom I never thought possible. No longer do I dread the end of the month, wondering if I'll have enough to cover my bills. No longer do I stress over the unknowns of a financial emergency. The sense of peace that comes with financial control has changed everything. It's not just about having enough money to pay the bills or living without debt—it's about the freedom to make choices based on what's important to me, rather than out of necessity. I've learned to live life on my own terms, and it's a feeling I want everyone to experience. The journey has been challenging, but each step forward has made it all worth it. Let me walk you through the milestones that made all the difference, the ones that reshaped my financial life and set me on the path to lasting success.

The Debt-Free Moment

The first big breakthrough in my financial journey was gaining control over my debt. If you've ever found yourself buried under a pile of high-interest credit card bills, personal loans, and car payments, you know exactly how suffocating it feels. That weight is constant, and it often keeps you up at night, wondering how you'll manage to pay everything off while still being able to cover daily expenses. The constant juggling act of making minimum payments while trying to avoid further financial disaster became a reality I was all too familiar with. But that all changed when I learned about velocity banking—a game-changing strategy that completely altered my approach to debt.

Velocity banking allowed me to pay off my high-interest car loan, consolidate credit card debt, and eliminate a personal loan that had been looming over me for years. It wasn't just about the numbers on a spreadsheet or feeling good about crossing things off a to-do list. It was a deep, emotional breakthrough. Getting rid of that debt was like lifting a fog that had clouded my thinking for years. It was the first time I truly felt free. I realized that debt wasn't just a financial burden—it was an emotional and mental weight that affected my well-being in ways I hadn't fully understood. When I became debt-free, I felt an overwhelming sense of relief. I was no longer a prisoner to my obligations. It wasn't just the satisfaction of paying off a bill; it was the mental clarity that came with it. I could finally breathe again, and it was a defining moment in my journey to financial freedom.

Building an Emergency Fund

The next crucial step in my financial transformation was building an emergency fund. Many people underestimate the importance of having a financial cushion, but let me tell you—it's a game-changer. When you don't have an emergency fund, every unexpected expense feels like a catastrophe. Whether it's a medical bill, a car repair, or a home appliance breaking down, it can throw your entire financial life into chaos if you're not prepared. That's why I made it a priority to save up a $15,000 emergency fund, putting it into a high-yield savings account where it could earn interest while being easily accessible if needed.

Having an emergency fund isn't just about having money in a savings account—it's about peace of mind. The security it offers changes how you approach life. For the first time, I felt confident that I could weather whatever life threw my way without panicking. I wasn't dependent on credit cards or loans to handle emergencies, and that made a huge difference in my overall financial health. But the emergency fund wasn't just a safety net—it became a growth tool. Every month, I watched it grow through the power of compound interest, and that gave me the confidence to take bigger steps toward financial growth. I saw it as my mini-retirement fund, quietly growing in the background, ensuring that I could handle life's curveballs without losing ground. The peace of mind it provided was priceless, allowing me to focus on the next steps in my journey without constantly worrying about financial setbacks.

Investing for the Future

Now comes the fun part—the magic of investing. This is where I learned that wealth isn't just about working harder or earning more; it's about making money work for you. For the longest time, I had been focused solely on earning a paycheck and paying down debt. But the moment I realized that investing was the key to building long-term wealth, everything clicked. Today, I make sure to max out both my Roth IRA and my wife's every year, knowing that these accounts are more than just retirement funds—they're the foundation of our financial security.

But investing doesn't stop there. I also opened a brokerage account, which is growing steadily thanks to consistent contributions and careful investment decisions. The key to investing is not just putting money in and forgetting about it—it's about learning how to make that money grow over time. One of the most powerful tools in investing is the magic of compound interest. I started reinvesting profits from dividends, and the more I did it, the more I saw the potential for long-term growth. Each time I log into my account and see the growth in my investments, I feel that rush of excitement. It's not about getting rich quick; it's about creating something that will last. The more I learned about how the stock market works and how different investments can build wealth, the more I understood that the real power comes from making your money work for you, not just the other way around. Every contribution, no matter how small, compounds over time and builds the foundation for a secure future. Watching my money grow has become one of the most rewarding aspects of this journey.

Making Money Work for Me

One of the most important lessons I've learned on this journey is that financial freedom isn't just about saving and investing—it's about creating streams of passive income. For years, I had been working hard for every dollar I earned, exchanging my time for money. But I knew that in order to achieve true financial independence, I needed to find ways to make money without always having to trade my time for it. That's when I started looking into passive income sources.

One of my first big ventures into passive income was investing in vending machines. Sounds unconventional, right? But it worked. I took on a little bit of debt to finance a few machines, placed them in high-traffic areas, and within seven months, the machines had paid for themselves and started generating monthly profits. That's passive income at its core—set it up, and it keeps earning for you without constant attention. It was a small start, but it proved that I could build systems that worked for me, not just the other way around. This initial success was the spark that made me look for other opportunities.

Next, I turned to the stock market, building a brokerage account that pays dividends and grows each year. By diversifying my investments, I began to see multiple streams of income coming in, reducing my reliance on any one source. This was the key: multiple income streams, whether from dividends, interest, or business ventures, provide financial security. It's like spreading your risk across different assets, ensuring that even if one source slows down, others continue to generate income. This strategy has helped me build a financial cushion that works for me, providing consistent cash flow without having to work for every dollar. The more I embraced passive income, the more I realized that financial freedom wasn't just about earning—it was about creating systems that generate wealth in the background.

Real Estate: The Long-Term Game

Real estate is the ultimate long-term play in my financial strategy. This is where I see the greatest opportunity for creating lasting wealth. While the stock market can provide solid returns, nothing beats the stability and growth potential of owning real estate. My goal before I retire from the military is to own 10 rental properties. It's a slow, deliberate process, but it's a strategy that compounds over time, much like any other long-term investment.

Each new property is another step toward creating a self-sustaining income that will allow me the freedom to focus on what really matters: my family, my passions, and continuing to grow my wealth. Real estate offers several key advantages—consistent cash flow, tax benefits, and property appreciation. As the market fluctuates, I've learned how to invest in undervalued areas with high potential for appreciation, making my properties more valuable over time. The best part? Real estate doesn't just provide immediate cash flow—it builds generational wealth. I'm not just thinking about my own future; I'm thinking about leaving something behind for my children and grandchildren. Whether I'm purchasing single-family homes, multi-unit properties, or commercial spaces, real estate allows me to create something tangible—assets that appreciate and produce income.

Real estate is the ultimate strategy for building long-term wealth. The strategy isn't about immediate gratification or flipping properties for a quick profit; it's about buying, holding, and building equity over time. As my portfolio grows, so does my ability to generate income without having to actively work for it. That's the beauty of real estate—it's a long-term game that provides not just financial returns, but the peace of mind that comes with owning valuable assets.

UNDERSTANDING VELOCITY BANKING AND THE POWER OF A PERSONAL LINE OF CREDIT (PLOC)

What is Velocity Banking?

Velocity Banking is a strategy that allows you to pay off debt much faster than traditional methods by leveraging a revolving line of credit, like a Personal Line of Credit (PLOC). This strategy focuses on reducing high-interest debts—like credit cards or car loans—by using the available credit of a PLOC, which offers lower interest rates compared to traditional forms of credit.

Let's break it down with a simple analogy: Imagine your finances as a river. Now, think of Velocity Banking as a dam that redirects the water (your cash flow) toward critical areas, like paying off high-interest debt. This redirection creates a flow of cash that helps you clear obstacles (your debts) quickly, eventually building a path toward financial freedom. Essentially, Velocity Banking isn't just about paying off debt at a slow pace—it's about strategically using your income and available credit to knock down the walls of financial stress and get ahead faster.

How Velocity Banking Works

At the core of Velocity Banking is the use of a Personal Line of Credit (PLOC) to pay down existing debt while managing your cash flow more efficiently. In a traditional debt-payoff strategy, you're focused on making minimum payments, and the process can drag on for years—especially if you're working with high-interest debt. With Velocity Banking, you borrow from your PLOC to pay off high-interest debt upfront, consolidating multiple debts into a single loan with a lower interest rate. This allows you to focus on paying down one balance instead of managing multiple debt sources with high interest rates.

A PLOC acts as a temporary bridge for your cash flow. Essentially, you borrow from the line of credit to pay off your high-interest debts, then, by depositing your income into the PLOC account, you gradually pay down the balance. Over time, this strategy not only helps you eliminate your debts faster, but it also reduces the total interest you pay. It's like putting the power of your income toward crushing the debt that's been holding you back, instead of letting it collect interest and grow.

Sara's Struggle with High-Interest Debt

Meet Sara. She's been working hard for years and has always paid her bills on time, but her credit card debt is a constant stress. She owes $10,000 on her credit cards with an interest rate of 18%. Every month, Sara makes the minimum payment of $200, but most of it goes toward paying interest rather than reducing the balance. At this rate, Sara feels like she's stuck in a financial treadmill, unable to make any significant progress.

One day, Sara learns about Velocity Banking and decides to take action. She applies for a Personal Line of Credit (PLOC) and is approved with a limit of $15,000 and a 6% interest rate. She uses this PLOC to pay off her entire $10,000 credit card balance, immediately reducing her interest rate from 18% to 6%. Instead of paying $180 each month in interest, she now only pays $50 in interest. That's a monthly savings of $130. Additionally, by using her PLOC, Sara can now focus on paying off the principal faster. Within just two years, she is able to eliminate the debt completely, saving thousands of dollars in interest.

By shifting from traditional minimum payments to Velocity Banking, Sara not only slashes the interest she's paying but also accelerates her debt repayment, which frees up money for other financial goals—like saving for a down payment on a house. Her financial stress reduces, and her sense of empowerment grows.

Offset Banking: Supercharging Velocity Banking

A crucial element of Velocity Banking is Offset Banking. This is a tactic where you deposit your paycheck directly into your PLOC instead of a standard checking account. This is a powerful way to reduce your debt, as it immediately lowers the balance on your PLOC. When your income is deposited into the PLOC, it temporarily reduces your available credit, and this reduction helps to minimize the interest you're charged.

To understand how this works, think of it like putting your cash flow into a system that automatically works to reduce your debt before it's even spent. In the traditional method, you might deposit your paycheck into a savings or checking account, only to later use that cash to make a payment on your debt. With Offset Banking, by using your income to reduce the balance of your PLOC immediately, you're effectively decreasing the interest owed before you start spending. This tactic can dramatically speed up your journey toward debt freedom.

James' Monthly Cash Flow Revolution

James, a single father, earns a solid salary of $4,500 a month. However, he's burdened by various debts, including a $7,000 personal loan at 12% interest, a $3,000 car loan at 8%, and $5,000 on a high-interest credit card. The interest is draining his finances, and he's frustrated with the idea of making minimum payments and seeing little to no progress.

After discovering Velocity Banking, James applies for a PLOC with a 7% interest rate and a limit of $15,000. He uses the PLOC to pay off his $7,000 personal loan and $5,000 credit card balance, consolidating all that high-interest debt into one loan. Now, instead of paying over $1,000 a year in interest, he's paying only $350. His monthly payment is much more manageable, and because he's able to deposit his paycheck directly into the PLOC, he's able to reduce the principal balance more quickly.

In just 18 months, James eliminates all his high-interest debts. The extra cash flow he generates allows him to not only pay off debt faster but also start building up an emergency savings fund. With Velocity Banking, he creates a path to financial security without the overwhelming burden of debt.

Why Traditional Debt Management Isn't Enough

Traditional Methods of Debt Repayment

When it comes to managing and paying off debt, two strategies usually dominate the conversation: the Debt Snowball and the Debt Avalanche. While both methods are effective, they each have their drawbacks when it comes to efficiently reducing interest and accelerating debt repayment.

- **Debt Snowball**: This method involves focusing on paying off the smallest debts first, regardless of their interest rates. While the emotional rewards are real, the method can be inefficient in terms of the amount of interest paid. Higher-interest debts, like credit cards, tend to linger for longer periods, making them more expensive over time.
- **Debt Avalanche**: This strategy focuses on paying off the highest-interest debt first. While this method saves money on interest over time, it can feel discouraging, especially when you're faced with large balances on high-interest debts. The progress may feel slow, leading to frustration.

Why Velocity Banking Works Better

Velocity Banking optimizes cash flow by using a PLOC to consolidate high-interest debt into one loan with a much lower interest rate. By using the full force of your income and available credit, you accelerate debt repayment, freeing up more of your cash flow for saving, investing, and pursuing other financial goals. Instead of simply making minimum payments, Velocity Banking ensures that your income is actively working to eliminate debt, allowing you to focus on building wealth faster.

The Power of a Personal Line of Credit (PLOC)

A Personal Line of Credit (PLOC) is a flexible, revolving line of credit that functions similarly to a credit card. However, it usually offers higher credit limits and lower interest rates than most credit cards, making it an ideal tool for consolidating high-interest debt and managing fluctuating cash flow. Essentially, a PLOC allows you to borrow money as needed, up to a specified limit, and pay it back over time.

Linda's Path to Financial Freedom

Linda, a small business owner, found herself constantly juggling personal and business debts. She had a personal loan at 14%, an outstanding credit card balance of $8,000 at 20% interest, and a business loan that was putting a strain on her cash flow. Linda struggled to manage everything and was barely making any headway in paying down the debt.

After learning about the PLOC, Linda decided to take the leap. She applied for one and used it to pay off both her personal loan and her credit card debt. Instead of paying 14% or 20% interest, she now paid 8% on the combined balance. Not only did this help her reduce her interest payments, but she also saved significantly on monthly costs.

By leveraging a PLOC and following the Velocity Banking strategy, Linda was able to consolidate her debt and redirect her payments towards eliminating the balance. Within two years, she was completely debt-free, giving her the breathing room she needed to reinvest in her business and grow her savings.

CONSOLIDATION AND ELIMINATION OF DEBT

Debt is often described as a heavy burden, and for many, it can feel like a weight that will never be lifted. The true cost of debt isn't just the amount owed but the interest you pay on that debt. Many people don't realize how much interest can accumulate over time, increasing the total cost of what they owe. In this chapter, we will break down the true cost of debt and explain how consolidation with tools like a Personal Line of Credit (PLOC) can provide a way to eliminate debt faster, save money, and allow you to regain control of your financial life. We'll also compare refinancing to debt consolidation, helping you understand which option works best for different situations. By walking through real-life examples, we'll see how Velocity Banking can dramatically accelerate your path to financial freedom by putting the power of debt elimination in your hands.

Why Interest is the Enemy

When you take out a loan or open a credit account, the interest rate attached to that loan is what makes paying it off so much harder. What many people don't realize is how much interest truly costs over time. For example, if you have a credit card with an 18% interest rate and a $10,000 balance, you could end up paying well over $5,000 in interest before the balance is paid off—if you're only making minimum payments. And this doesn't even consider the compounding interest, where you end up paying interest on your interest. This phenomenon is particularly dangerous because it keeps you in debt longer and costs you more than you originally borrowed.

Interest isn't just a number on a statement—it's a silent drain on your wealth. Consider this: the longer you stay in debt, the more you'll pay in interest. High-interest debts like credit cards, student loans, car loans, and personal loans can carry rates of 10% or higher. This means you're potentially throwing away hundreds, if not thousands, of dollars each year just on the interest. Many people find themselves trapped in a cycle where only a fraction of their monthly payments goes toward the actual debt, with the rest swallowed up by interest.

By focusing on eliminating high-interest debt first, you can begin to take back control of your finances. Reducing interest costs frees up more of your monthly budget, allowing you to apply more money to the principal balance. This helps you pay off your debt faster, break free from the financial stranglehold, and start building wealth.

Refinancing vs. Consolidation with a PLOC

When people first consider tackling their debt, one of the first strategies they encounter is refinancing. Refinancing involves taking out a new loan to pay off existing debt, typically at a lower interest rate. It can seem like an attractive option, especially when the new loan offers a much lower rate than the old one, which can help you reduce your overall interest payments. However, refinancing isn't always the best choice. While it may seem like a simple solution, refinancing can come with hidden costs, such as origination fees, closing costs, or prepayment penalties. Additionally, refinancing may extend the life of your loan, meaning you end up paying more over the long term, even with the lower interest rate.

Refinancing can also take a while to process. While you wait for approval, your existing debt continues to accrue interest, potentially causing you to pay more than anticipated by the time your new loan comes through. And if you have less-than-perfect credit, you might not even qualify for the best rates, leaving you in a position that's not much better than before.

This is where consolidation with a Personal Line of Credit (PLOC) becomes a game-changer. A PLOC offers a faster, more flexible alternative to refinancing. Instead of dealing with long approval processes, closing fees, or refinancing paperwork, a PLOC lets you consolidate your debt into one manageable, lower-interest payment. With a PLOC, you use the available credit to pay off high-interest loans, credit cards, and other debts at a significantly lower interest rate than the one you're currently paying. This immediate reduction in your interest rate can help you pay off your debt much faster, saving you money in the long run.

The key benefit of a PLOC is that it gives you the flexibility to manage your debt while taking advantage of lower interest rates. You'll have fewer monthly bills to manage, making it easier to stay on track and avoid missing payments, which could further harm your credit score. Since you can withdraw funds as needed and only pay interest on the balance you carry, the PLOC provides the flexibility to adjust your payments according to your cash flow.

Real-Life Example: Debt Consolidation and Elimination

Let's take a closer look at a real-life example of how debt consolidation using a PLOC can dramatically change your financial trajectory. Meet Sarah. Sarah has a total of $30,000 in debt, spread across three high-interest obligations: a $15,000 credit card with 18% APR, a $10,000 personal loan at 12%, and a $5,000 car loan at 7%. At first glance, Sarah feels overwhelmed by her debt. She makes minimum payments on her credit card and car loan, but her balances hardly move. With her personal loan, the interest alone is more than $100 per month.

Sarah decides to take action and explores debt consolidation through a PLOC. After researching various options, she opens a Personal Line of Credit with a 10% interest rate. Here's how it works:

1. **Consolidation**: Sarah uses her PLOC to pay off her credit card, personal loan, and car loan in full. The 10% interest rate on the PLOC is much lower than the interest rates on her previous debts, immediately reducing her overall interest burden.
2. **Cash Flow Optimization**: By consolidating her debts into one payment, Sarah's monthly bills become simpler to manage. Instead of having to remember three different payment dates and amounts, she now has one streamlined payment. The best part is that her PLOC payment is much lower than the sum of her old minimum payments. This gives her more room in her budget to focus on paying down the principal balance.
3. **Accelerated Payoff**: With Sarah's new payment structure, she starts putting her extra cash into the PLOC. By depositing her paycheck directly into the PLOC each month, Sarah reduces her average daily balance. This means she pays less interest on her

balance, accelerating her debt repayment. Using Velocity Banking strategies, Sarah is able to pay down her debt faster than she would have with traditional repayment methods.

Within two years, Sarah has paid off the $30,000 in debt. What would have taken her nearly eight years under her old repayment plan was achieved in less than two years thanks to debt consolidation with a PLOC. The extra money she saves on interest gets reinvested into her PLOC, helping her pay down the principal faster. Her financial outlook is now brighter, and she has learned the power of leveraging lower-interest debt to her advantage.

How Consolidation Through PLOC Empowers You

Sarah's success story is a powerful reminder that consolidating your debt through a PLOC isn't just about reducing interest payments—it's about gaining control over your financial future. When you consolidate multiple debts into one, you simplify your finances and free up more of your income to focus on what matters most: paying off your debt and building wealth. Consolidating debt can be a catalyst for change, helping you reduce financial stress and give you the peace of mind to look ahead.

By consolidating debt into a single line of credit, you're not just managing multiple payments; you're taking proactive steps toward long-term financial health. This is especially empowering because a PLOC allows you to make every dollar work for you. When you deposit your paycheck directly into your PLOC, your available balance decreases, reducing the interest you're charged. This technique, known as "Offset Banking," allows you to pay down debt at a much faster rate than traditional methods.

The power of Velocity Banking lies in this approach.

Traditional debt repayment methods are often slow and tedious, with interest eating up the majority of your payments. But with a PLOC, you're leveraging your cash flow to dramatically reduce your debt faster, giving you more flexibility and control over your financial future.

The Ultimate Goal—Financial Freedom

The ultimate goal of consolidating and eliminating debt isn't just about paying off balances. It's about creating the freedom to live life on your terms. Once you eliminate high-interest debt, the money that would have gone toward interest payments can be redirected into wealth-building endeavors like investing in retirement accounts, building an emergency fund, or even saving for major life goals like buying a home or funding a child's education.

The beauty of debt elimination tools like Velocity Banking is that they give you a clear, actionable path to freedom. You don't have to spend decades stuck in a cycle of debt. By consolidating your debts, optimizing your cash flow, and focusing on paying down your principal quickly, you can put yourself on a path to financial success much sooner than you might think.

As your debts disappear, you open the door to new financial possibilities. You can now focus on investing, growing your wealth, and preparing for the future without the cloud of debt looming overhead. Velocity Banking isn't just a way to pay off debt; it's a strategy for achieving long-term financial freedom.

In this chapter, we've explored how consolidating your debt with a PLOC can reduce your interest costs, simplify your payments, and accelerate your path to financial freedom. By prioritizing high-interest debts and leveraging tools like Velocity Banking, you can regain control over your finances and create a future where wealth-building becomes the focus, rather than just debt repayment. As demonstrated through Sarah's real-life example, consolidating debt with a PLOC is not just about reducing debt—it's about taking action to empower yourself and position your finances for long-term success. With the right strategies, you can break free from debt and start building the life you've always dreamed of.

GAINING ASSETS THROUGH VELOCITY BANKING

After using Velocity Banking to eliminate debt, it's time to pivot towards building long-term wealth. This phase is crucial because it's not just about getting out of debt, but about creating a sustainable financial future. In this section, we'll explore how Velocity Banking doesn't just stop at helping you eliminate debt but can also serve as a powerful tool for acquiring valuable assets that generate wealth over time. By strategically reallocating the money you've freed up from high-interest debt into income-producing assets, you can create streams of passive income that provide long-term financial security.

The money saved from paying off credit card debt, personal loans, and other high-interest liabilities can be reinvested into opportunities that continue to work for you, whether it's real estate, investments, or building a business. The transition from paying off debt to investing in assets is where your financial journey truly begins. With the right mindset and strategy, you'll be able to take the financial discipline you've developed through Velocity Banking and turn it into wealth-building momentum. Whether you're interested in securing a profitable real estate portfolio, growing an investment portfolio, or launching a business that provides ongoing revenue, Velocity Banking provides the flexibility and resources you need to make those dreams a reality.

Ultimately, this chapter will show how Velocity Banking, when applied with intention and consistency, can propel you toward the goal of financial independence, setting you up for a future where your wealth continues to grow, even as you sleep.

The Importance of Acquiring Assets

When it comes to building long-term wealth, the foundation lies in acquiring assets. Assets are anything that puts money in your pocket, whether it's real estate, stocks, bonds, or businesses. These are the building blocks of financial freedom, as they generate income without requiring your constant labor. On the other hand, liabilities are things that take money out of your pocket, such as credit card debt, car loans, or even your personal residence if you're not using it strategically. The key to achieving financial freedom is to focus on accumulating assets while minimizing liabilities.

Velocity Banking provides a unique approach to acquiring assets. By freeing up money that would otherwise go toward high-interest debt, you can use those funds to invest in income-generating assets that will work for you. The first step is understanding how Velocity Banking works to minimize your liabilities and convert them into tools for acquiring assets. For example, once your high-interest debt is cleared, you can use the cash flow to build an emergency fund, invest in stocks, or acquire real estate that generates consistent cash flow.

This strategic shift from paying off debt to acquiring assets is the difference between working for money and having money work for you. The idea is to continuously funnel the money you would have spent on interest payments into investments that compound and grow, allowing you to build wealth over time.

As you begin to accumulate more assets, it's important to remember that the real power of wealth-building comes from diversification. While a single income-producing asset, like a rental property or stocks, can certainly help, the true potential for building wealth lies in holding multiple assets that work in harmony. Real estate might appreciate in value, but stocks can provide dividend income that grows each year. Having a diversified portfolio of assets ensures that your financial future is more secure, with multiple streams of income feeding into your wealth-building strategy.

Detailed Example: Let's consider Sarah, who paid off her $30,000 credit card debt using Velocity Banking. By reducing her monthly interest payments, Sarah has freed up $600 each month. She decides to invest this saved cash flow into a diversified stock portfolio. Over time, her portfolio grows at an average annual return of 7%, and within 10 years, the $600 invested each month turns into over $100,000. Had Sarah kept paying off debt at the minimum payments, she would have been stuck in that cycle, and wouldn't have seen her money grow in this way. Instead, Velocity Banking empowered her to use that money to generate assets that work for her long term.

Real Estate: A Wealth-Building Vehicle

Real estate is one of the most powerful tools for building wealth, and Velocity Banking can be a game-changer when it comes to acquiring property. Real estate offers two main benefits that make it an attractive investment: cash flow and appreciation. When you own rental properties, they generate cash flow through monthly rent payments. As time passes, properties tend to appreciate in value, increasing your net worth.

The beauty of real estate is that it can serve as both an income stream and an equity-building vehicle. Not only are you collecting rent, but as the mortgage is paid down, you're building equity. Over time, this can provide you with a significant asset base that can be leveraged for further investments or eventually be sold for a lump sum profit. This combination of ongoing cash flow and growing equity makes real estate one of the most reliable ways to build long-term wealth.

Velocity Banking can be used to acquire real estate by leveraging debt wisely. By using a PLOC or a Home Equity Line of Credit (HELOC), you can acquire properties without having to tie up all of your savings or retirement funds. Leveraging debt means using borrowed money to finance the purchase of an asset, allowing you to retain more of your cash to keep building your portfolio. While debt can be risky, Velocity Banking minimizes that risk by focusing on strategic debt management—ensuring that you're paying off the debt quickly and efficiently, all while using your properties to generate positive cash flow.

One of the most compelling ways Velocity Banking works with real estate is that it allows you to accelerate the debt payoff on the properties you acquire. Instead of being stuck in traditional mortgage payments that last 15 to 30 years, Velocity Banking allows you to funnel more money into the property's debt, paying it down faster and freeing up cash flow sooner. This is particularly helpful when dealing with multiple properties, as the quicker the debt is paid off, the more income you have to reinvest in additional properties, creating a snowball effect.

Imagine you have a PLOC with a $100,000 limit, and you use this credit line to purchase a rental property for $90,000. Your monthly mortgage payment is $500, and the property generates $1,200 in rent. After accounting for expenses, such as taxes and maintenance, you make $400 a month in net cash flow. This means you're able to use the rental income to pay down the PLOC balance while also generating wealth. After a few years, the value of the property increases, and you can either sell for a profit or refinance to acquire additional properties.

The more properties you acquire using Velocity Banking, the faster your portfolio grows. The key is to focus on acquiring properties that generate positive cash flow—properties that not only pay for themselves but also generate income that can be used to accelerate your debt repayments and further grow your portfolio. Eventually, this income and equity will give you the financial freedom to make other investments or retire early.

Real estate doesn't just build personal wealth—it can help create generational wealth for your family. As you acquire more properties, you're laying the groundwork for a legacy that will provide financial security for future generations. By strategically using Velocity Banking to grow your real estate holdings, you're setting up a financial foundation that extends beyond your lifetime. This ability to create wealth that lasts across generations is one of the most powerful aspects of real estate investing.

Building Passive Income Streams

One of the most transformative concepts in the pursuit of financial independence is the idea of passive income. Passive income refers to money earned with little to no active involvement once the initial work has been done. Instead of working for money, you have money working for you. It's about eliminating the need to trade hours for dollars, allowing you to create streams of income that continue to flow even when you're not working. Passive income is the ultimate goal of financial freedom, and it can come from many sources. Whether it's from investments, automated businesses, or creative endeavors, passive income allows you to focus on enjoying life and growing your wealth, rather than working constantly for a paycheck.

When you incorporate Velocity Banking into the mix, you get access to the financial flexibility that's crucial for creating passive income streams. By using the money you've freed up through eliminating high-interest debt, you can invest in opportunities that require little to no work on your part but continue to provide returns.

Stocks and Dividends: The stock market offers one of the most effective ways to build wealth over time. By investing in dividend-paying stocks, you can earn a regular stream of passive income from the dividends paid out by these companies. These dividends can be reinvested into more shares of stock, compounding your wealth even faster. Over time, your portfolio grows, and your monthly or quarterly dividend payouts increase. You're able to put your money into investments that work for you, providing returns while requiring little to no work on your part.

A smart, long-term investment strategy in the stock market can result in significant growth. Let's say you invest $500 each month into a diversified portfolio of dividend-paying stocks. If your stocks return an average of 6%

annually, your $500 monthly contribution could grow to over $100,000 in 10 years, even without accounting for reinvested dividends. Over the long term, stock prices typically increase, leading to capital appreciation, while dividends offer a steady income stream.

Side Hustles and Vending Machines: While stocks and real estate are fantastic vehicles for wealth-building, it's important to recognize that passive income can also be generated from unconventional sources that require little to no work. For example, vending machines and ATMs are excellent tools to generate passive income. These businesses require an upfront investment and some initial setup, but after that, they operate largely on their own, producing income with minimal effort.

I personally have a small fleet of vending machines and ATM machines, and they generate anywhere from $400 to $1,000 per month, depending on the location and products offered. I've placed these machines in high-traffic areas, such as offices, gyms, and apartment buildings, where people are always looking for snacks, drinks, or cash. The key to success is selecting the right location and products—once you've made those decisions, the income starts rolling in with very little maintenance required. The money you make from vending or ATM machines can be reinvested into more machines, helping you grow your

HOME EQUITY LINE OF CREDIT (HELOC)

In this section, we will delve into advanced strategies and tools that can help you fast-track your journey to financial freedom. While we have already covered the basics of Velocity Banking, there are additional options available that can significantly accelerate your wealth-building process. These tools empower you to optimize the financial resources at your disposal, allowing you to strategically reduce debt, increase investments, and ultimately build lasting wealth. One of the most powerful tools available for this is the Home Equity Line of Credit (HELOC). A HELOC offers a unique opportunity to tap into the equity of your home—a valuable asset that, for many homeowners, is the largest source of untapped wealth. By leveraging the equity in your home, you can access flexible funds with lower interest rates than traditional credit products. In this chapter, we'll explore how a HELOC works, how it compares to other financial tools like the Personal Line of Credit (PLOC), and how to use it strategically to pay off debt faster, acquire more assets, and generate long-term wealth. Whether you're looking to consolidate high-interest debt, invest in income-producing properties, or improve your financial position, a HELOC can be a key tool to accelerate your journey to financial independence.

What is a HELOC and How Does It Work?

A Home Equity Line of Credit (HELOC) is a type of revolving credit that allows homeowners to borrow against the equity in their homes. This tool is powerful because it essentially enables you to leverage the value of your home, which is often one of your most significant assets. Home equity refers to the difference between the current market value of your home and the amount you still owe on your mortgage. For instance, if your home is appraised at $300,000 and you owe $150,000 on your mortgage, you have $150,000 in equity. A HELOC enables you to borrow against that equity, typically up to 85% of your home's value, depending on your creditworthiness and other financial factors. The amount you can borrow is determined based on the available equity in your home, but the real power comes from how you can access and use that equity. A HELOC works similarly to a credit card, offering you flexibility and access to cash when you need it. Whether you're looking to pay off high-interest debt, invest in income-generating assets, or fund major purchases or improvements, a HELOC gives you the financial flexibility to make those decisions without having to rely on more expensive or less flexible loans. What makes a HELOC particularly attractive is the way it can be used to free up cash flow, which you can reinvest into wealth-building strategies. This could mean reinvesting into income-producing assets like real estate or using the saved money to build emergency funds, create business opportunities, or accelerate the payment of high-interest debt.

What sets a HELOC apart from other financial tools like

personal loans or credit cards is its structure and the way it works. A HELOC is a revolving credit line, similar to a credit card. This means you can borrow money, repay it, and then borrow again, up to the credit limit, as long as you're within the terms of the agreement. This flexibility is one of the reasons why a HELOC is such a powerful tool for debt elimination and wealth-building. You don't have to worry about getting a lump-sum loan, which would require you to repay the full amount over time. Instead, the funds are available as needed, offering you the ability to access your equity when you need it the most, while still retaining the option to borrow more if needed.

HELOCs generally come with two distinct phases:

Draw Period (typically 5-10 years)
During this time, you can borrow funds up to your credit limit, and you are typically only required to make interest-only payments. The ability to borrow and only pay interest on the amount you use can provide you with significant cash flow flexibility. This is particularly beneficial when you're using the HELOC to pay off high-interest debts or invest in assets. As you make payments during this phase, your available credit replenishes, and you can continue borrowing within your credit limit, as long as you remain current on the loan.

Additionally, the interest-only payments are often set at a lower rate compared to credit cards or personal loans, meaning you'll be paying much less in interest. For homeowners looking to accelerate debt repayment or invest in income-producing assets, this low-interest period can be invaluable in terms of cash flow. For instance, if you're using a HELOC to consolidate higher-interest debt, the extra money you save in interest payments can be redirected into other financial ventures. You can strategically pay down credit card debt with the HELOC, giving you more disposable income, which could then be used for investments that provide ongoing passive income, such as rental properties or dividend stocks.

Repayment Period (10-20 years)

After the draw period ends, you will transition into the repayment period, where you'll need to start repaying both the principal and the interest, usually with a fixed payment schedule. While your monthly payment may increase during this time, the flexibility of the initial draw period still provides room to use the HELOC for wealth-building or debt consolidation purposes. The repayment period typically lasts between 10 and 20 years, giving you a structured timeline to pay off the loan.

One of the major advantages of a HELOC is its lower interest rates compared to other forms of borrowing, like credit cards or personal loans. Interest rates on HELOCs can range from 6% to 8%, while credit card interest rates typically start around 18% and can go much higher. This makes HELOCs an attractive option for consolidating high-interest debts, allowing you to save significant money on interest over time. The funds you save can then be directed toward investing in assets that appreciate over time, building your wealth and advancing your financial goals. The ability to borrow at a lower rate makes a HELOC an ideal solution for people looking to get out of debt while still generating wealth.

For example, let's say you have $20,000 in credit card debt, which carries an interest rate of 18%. Using a HELOC, you can consolidate that debt at a much lower interest rate of, say, 6%. By transferring your credit card debt to the HELOC, you immediately save money on interest payments. If you were paying $400 a month in interest on the credit card debt, you might find that your interest payments drop to $150 per month on the HELOC, freeing up $250 every month. That $250 in savings can then be redirected toward other financial priorities, such as building an emergency fund, investing, or making additional principal payments on the HELOC.

Another key benefit of a HELOC is its flexibility in how you use the funds. You don't have to use the entire amount at once; you can borrow funds as needed, depending on your financial situation and goals. Whether you use the HELOC to pay off high-interest debts, invest in income-generating assets like real estate, or make improvements to your home to increase its value, the HELOC offers a wide range of applications. This flexibility can give you the confidence to use your equity strategically while not being locked into any one type of investment.

Leveraging Your Home Equity for Wealth Building The real power of a HELOC, however, comes when you use it to acquire income-generating assets. For example, once you pay off your high-interest debt, you can use the funds from your HELOC to invest in real estate properties, stocks, or businesses that generate positive cash flow. Real estate investments are particularly attractive because they can provide a steady stream of passive income and appreciation over time.

Real estate is a particularly attractive option for many homeowners using a HELOC to accelerate wealth-building. By leveraging your home equity, you can purchase rental properties that generate passive income, allowing you to cover the costs of the HELOC and still create additional streams of revenue. Not only does this help you build wealth through appreciation, but it also provides a steady cash flow, which can then be reinvested into additional properties, creating a snowball effect. This process allows you to use the profits from your properties to pay down the HELOC and ultimately increase your equity, positioning you to make more investments down the line.

In summary, a HELOC is a versatile and powerful tool for debt elimination and wealth-building. Its lower interest rates, combined with its revolving credit structure, provide you with financial flexibility that can be strategically leveraged to achieve long-term financial goals. Whether used to pay off high-interest debts, acquire income-generating assets, or invest in opportunities that build equity over time, a HELOC can significantly accelerate your journey to financial freedom and wealth creation.

HELOC vs. PLOC

While both a Home Equity Line of Credit (HELOC) and a Personal Line of Credit (PLOC) provide access to credit, they differ in several significant ways that can influence when and how each one is best used. Understanding these differences is crucial when deciding which financial tool to use to achieve your goals. Below is a breakdown of the key differences between a HELOC and a PLOC:

HELOC

A Home Equity Line of Credit (HELOC) is a secured line of credit, meaning that your home acts as collateral. The amount you can borrow through a HELOC is based on the equity in your home, which is the difference between the current market value of the property and the amount you owe on your mortgage. Since the loan is secured by real property, lenders are more likely to offer lower interest rates compared to unsecured credit products. This makes a HELOC ideal for larger borrowing needs, such as consolidating high-interest debt, funding real estate investments, or paying down your mortgage faster.

Advantages of a HELOC:
- Lower interest rates compared to unsecured loans like credit cards or personal loans.
- Larger borrowing capacity due to the collateral (your home).
- Flexibility to borrow, repay, and borrow again up to the credit limit during the draw period.
- Potential for tax deductions on interest payments when used for home improvement or investment purposes (consult a tax professional).
- Longer repayment terms in most cases, which can help manage larger loans over a more extended period.

Risks of a HELOC:
- Your home is at risk if you fail to repay the loan. Since your home is used as collateral, a default could lead to foreclosure.
- Your borrowing capacity is limited to the equity in your home. If your home's value drops, your borrowing limit may decrease.
- Interest rates can be variable, which means your payments could increase if market rates rise.
- Temporarily increasing debt—Since the interest-only payments are often an option during the draw period, there is a risk of accumulating more debt than initially planned.

PLOC

A Personal Line of Credit (PLOC), on the other hand, is an unsecured line of credit, meaning that it does not require collateral. The lender evaluates your creditworthiness, income, and other financial factors to determine your borrowing limit. Because the loan is unsecured, PLOCs tend to have higher interest rates than HELOCs. PLOCs are best suited for short-term financial needs, smaller amounts of credit, or emergency situations where you don't want to risk your property.

Advantages of a PLOC:
- No collateral required, which means your home or assets are not at risk if you fail to repay the loan.
- Faster application process and less paperwork than a HELOC since there's no need for an appraisal of your home's value.
- Flexible use for ongoing expenses, emergency needs, or small-scale investments.
- Simplified repayment structure, as most PLOCs come with fixed repayment schedules after the draw period, making them easier to manage for short-term debts.

Risks of a PLOC:
- Higher interest rates than HELOCs, often starting at 10% and going higher depending on your credit profile.
- Lower borrowing limits because the credit is unsecured. Since there is no collateral involved, lenders typically offer less borrowing capacity.
- Limited use for large investments or long-term financial strategies, as the interest payments can become prohibitively high.

Choosing Between a HELOC and a PLOC

In terms of choosing between a HELOC and a PLOC, the key factors to consider are the amount of debt you need to consolidate, the size of the investment you want to make, and the timeline for repayment. If you are planning a large, long-term project—such as real estate investment or consolidating substantial credit card debt—a HELOC is likely the better option. Its lower interest rates, larger borrowing limits, and potential tax advantages make it an ideal choice for financing significant ventures and building long-term wealth.

On the other hand, if you have short-term needs or are seeking smaller amounts of credit, a PLOC may be more appropriate. It's quicker to access and doesn't put your home at risk. A PLOC is useful for covering smaller expenses or emergencies, such as medical bills, car repairs, or other unexpected financial needs, where you don't want to tie up your home as collateral.

Additionally, many people use a PLOC to smooth out cash flow during uncertain times, such as a job transition or unexpected medical expenses. Since there are no collateral requirements and the application process is often more streamlined, a PLOC is ideal for individuals who need quick access to credit without the extended paperwork or risk associated with a HELOC.

Ultimately, the choice between a HELOC and a PLOC depends on your financial goals, risk tolerance, and the amount of debt or credit you need to access. HELOCs are ideal for those seeking larger sums of money with a plan to invest and build wealth, while PLOCs serve as a flexible tool for more immediate, smaller-scale financial needs.

Using a HELOC to Pay Off Your Mortgage and Acquire More Real Estate

One of the most powerful uses for a Home Equity Line of Credit (HELOC) is to accelerate the payoff of your mortgage or fund new real estate investments. By using the equity in your home, you can significantly reduce your mortgage balance and increase your wealth-building potential by acquiring additional income-producing assets, such as rental properties. A HELOC provides you with a revolving credit line, allowing you to borrow and repay funds, which makes it an ideal tool for improving cash flow and creating new opportunities for growth.

Using a HELOC in this way can not only free up cash flow but also generate long-term passive income by acquiring rental properties that appreciate over time. You can strategically deploy the funds from a HELOC to pay down your mortgage faster, invest in real estate, and leverage the equity in your home to continually build your wealth.

Let's walk through a real-world example that illustrates how you can use a HELOC to accelerate your mortgage payoff and grow your real estate portfolio.

Using a HELOC to Pay Off Your Mortgage and Acquire Rental Properties

Imagine you're a homeowner named Sarah. You've been living in your home for several years and, thanks to the rising property values, you've built up a significant amount of equity. Let's break down Sarah's financial situation and how she leverages a HELOC to pay down her mortgage and grow her wealth.

Sarah's Financial Overview:
- Current Home Value: $350,000
- Mortgage Balance: $150,000
- Equity in Home: $200,000 (the difference between her home's value and her mortgage balance)
- HELOC Credit Limit: $170,000 (based on 85% of her home's equity)

Sarah has worked hard to pay down her mortgage, and she's built up a nice nest egg of home equity. But now she's ready to accelerate her wealth-building efforts. Rather than sitting on the equity in her home, she decides to use it strategically by taking out a HELOC and paying off her mortgage faster while also venturing into real estate investing.

Step 1: Using the HELOC to Pay Off the Mortgage

Sarah opens a HELOC with a $170,000 limit, which means she has access to a significant amount of her home's equity. The HELOC gives her the ability to borrow, repay, and borrow again. Sarah takes advantage of this flexibility to pay down her mortgage.

She decides to use $100,000 from the HELOC to pay off a large chunk of her mortgage balance. Here's how this works:

- Original Mortgage: $150,000
- Amount Paid Using HELOC: $100,000
- New Mortgage Balance: $50,000

By using the HELOC to pay down her mortgage, Sarah has reduced her mortgage balance from $150,000 to just $50,000. Not only has she freed up extra cash flow (since her mortgage payment is now lower), but she's also paying less interest overall because the HELOC interest rate is 6%, compared to the 4.5% rate on her original mortgage.

This is a smart move because the interest on the HELOC is lower than her original mortgage, allowing her to save money over time. The best part is that Sarah can continue using the HELOC to borrow money and pay off more of her mortgage, depending on how much equity she wants to leverage.

Step 2: Using the HELOC to Acquire Rental Properties

Now that Sarah has paid down a large portion of her mortgage, she wants to start acquiring income-producing assets—specifically, rental properties. She knows that real estate is a proven wealth-building tool, and by using the funds from her HELOC, she can acquire new properties without selling her existing investments or tapping into her savings.

Sarah decides to use $100,000 from the HELOC to purchase her first rental property. She finds a 3-bedroom, 2-bathroom house in a growing neighborhood listed for $250,000. With a 20% down payment requirement, she uses the $100,000 from the HELOC to cover the down payment and closing costs, leaving her with a mortgage balance of $200,000 on the property.

Step 3: Managing Cash Flow from the Rental Property

The rental property generates $2,500 per month in rental income. After accounting for the property's mortgage payment of $1,200, property management fees of $300, insurance, taxes, and maintenance costs, Sarah is left with $800 in positive cash flow each month.

Sarah decides to use this $800 cash flow to pay down the balance of her HELOC. By making extra payments with this rental income, she is able to pay off the HELOC faster, reducing her debt more quickly and keeping the cycle of leveraging debt and building wealth moving forward.

Here's a breakdown of Sarah's monthly cash flow situation after the rental property:
- Rental Income: $2,500
- Mortgage Payment: $1,200
- Other Expenses (property management, insurance, taxes, etc.): $500
- Net Cash Flow: $800

Sarah takes that $800 per month and applies it toward paying off her HELOC, allowing her to reduce the balance faster. Over time, as her mortgage payment is reduced, she will pay down the HELOC more quickly, freeing up more funds to reinvest into additional properties or pay down her primary mortgage.

Step 4: Scaling the Real Estate Portfolio

As Sarah continues to pay down her HELOC, her equity in both her primary residence and the rental property grows. In three years, her rental property has appreciated in value by 10%, bringing its market value to $275,000. At the same time, Sarah has used rental income to reduce her HELOC balance, and now she's ready to take the next step.

Sarah uses her growing equity to purchase another rental property. This time, she's able to use the $70,000 in available HELOC funds to cover the down payment on a second property, which she purchases for $200,000. The second rental property generates similar monthly cash flow, and Sarah now has two rental properties producing income and paying down her HELOC simultaneously.

Step 5: The Snowball Effect of Leveraging HELOC Funds

Over the next few years, Sarah continues to acquire more rental properties, each time using her HELOC to fund the down payments and scaling her portfolio. The more properties she owns, the more rental income she generates. This income can either be used to pay down the HELOC faster or be reinvested into more properties.

In addition to the cash flow and tax benefits of real estate, Sarah is also benefiting from the appreciation in property values. As her properties increase in value and the debt on her HELOC decreases, her net worth grows significantly.

Summary of Sarah's Strategy

- Initial HELOC Borrowing: Sarah used her HELOC to pay down her mortgage by $100,000, reducing her debt burden.
- Real Estate Investment: Sarah then used the same

HELOC to purchase rental properties, generating cash flow and building her wealth.
- Cash Flow Management: The rental income is used to pay down her HELOC, freeing up more funds to reinvest in real estate.
- Portfolio Growth: Sarah uses the power of compound growth by reinvesting the profits into more real estate, accelerating her wealth-building efforts.

By leveraging her home's equity, Sarah was able to break free from the traditional cycle of only paying off debt. Instead, she built a real estate portfolio that generates passive income, increasing her wealth while paying down the debt she incurred to finance the properties.

The Power of Using a HELOC for Real Estate Investing

Sarah's example is a prime illustration of how using a HELOC can turbocharge your wealth-building efforts. By leveraging the equity in your home to pay off your mortgage and acquire rental properties, you can accelerate debt repayment and build a portfolio of income-generating assets. This strategy not only helps you reduce your liabilities, but it also creates a growing stream of passive income that can eventually provide financial freedom.

Real estate is an incredibly effective long-term wealth-building tool, and with the help of a HELOC, you can capitalize on opportunities without needing to tie up a significant amount of cash. The ability to borrow, repay, and borrow again means that you have a flexible and powerful tool at your disposal to accelerate your financial growth.

Using a PLOC to Pay Down Your Mortgage Faster, Then Transitioning to a HELOC

In addition to using a Home Equity Line of Credit (HELOC), another powerful strategy to accelerate your mortgage payoff is by using a Personal Line of Credit (PLOC). A PLOC is an unsecured line of credit that can offer you financial flexibility and a way to reduce your mortgage balance faster than by adhering to the standard amortization schedule. When used correctly, a PLOC allows you to make lump-sum payments toward the principal of your mortgage, which results in a reduced loan balance and, more importantly, a significant reduction in the amount of interest paid over the life of the loan. This method of leveraging credit can accelerate the pace of your financial freedom journey.

While the concept may seem simple—use the PLOC to pay down the principal more quickly—the strategy requires understanding your mortgage structure, recognizing how your payments are applied, and taking full advantage of the power of lump-sum contributions. Below, we will break down how this strategy works in detail, step by step, and how it can set you up for a smoother transition to even more advanced debt reduction techniques like using a HELOC.

Step 1: Review Your Amortization Schedule

The first step in using a PLOC to pay down your mortgage faster is to thoroughly review your existing mortgage amortization schedule. Your amortization schedule provides a detailed breakdown of your mortgage payments over time, showing you how much of each payment goes toward interest and how much is applied to the principal balance.

In the early years of a mortgage, especially if you have a long-term loan, the majority of your payments will be applied toward paying off the interest, rather than the principal. This is due to the way amortization works: because the interest is calculated on the remaining balance, early payments mostly cover the interest charges. As a result, it takes a long time to significantly reduce the principal balance, even if you make regular payments.

This is where the magic of lump-sum payments comes into play. By paying extra toward your principal, you reduce the balance that interest is calculated on, which in turn lowers the total amount of interest you'll pay over the life of the loan. For example, if you have a mortgage balance of $200,000, most of your early payments may go toward interest, meaning your principal balance remains relatively high. However, by applying a lump-sum payment—say $50,000 from a PLOC—you immediately reduce that $200,000 balance, which allows a greater portion of your monthly payments to be applied to the remaining principal rather than interest.

This strategy requires you to understand the impact of these lump-sum payments and how they alter the amortization schedule. The more you pay toward the principal, the more quickly you can reduce the interest burden. Essentially, you're speeding up the process of becoming debt-free.

Step 2: Use a PLOC for Lump-Sum Payments

Now that you have reviewed your amortization schedule and understand how your payments are structured, the next step is to leverage a PLOC for making lump-sum payments toward your mortgage. Let's break down this step with a real-world example to demonstrate how you can use a PLOC effectively.

Suppose you have a mortgage balance of $200,000, and you have access to a PLOC with a limit of $50,000. Instead of continuing to make the traditional mortgage payments, you

can use the PLOC to make a substantial lump-sum payment directly toward the principal. Let's say you take $50,000 from your PLOC and apply it to the mortgage principal.
- Original Mortgage Balance: $200,000
- PLOC Payment: $50,000
- New Mortgage Balance: $150,000

By reducing your mortgage balance to $150,000, you've already made a significant dent in the total amount of interest you'll pay over the life of the loan. The reason this strategy works is that your monthly mortgage payment is still the same, but now that your mortgage balance is lower, a larger portion of your payment will go toward the principal rather than the interest. Over time, this creates a compounding effect, allowing you to pay off your mortgage faster.

The PLOC has allowed you to effectively accelerate the repayment process by shifting the focus from interest-heavy payments to principal-heavy payments. If you continue this process over time, applying any extra funds toward the mortgage principal whenever possible, you can significantly shorten the term of your mortgage and save thousands of dollars in interest payments.

Step 3: Recalculate Your New Amortization Schedule

Once you've made a lump-sum payment toward your mortgage using the PLOC, it's essential to recalculate your new amortization schedule to reflect the updated mortgage balance. The recalculation will show you how your monthly payments are now being applied and the impact the lump-sum payment has had on your mortgage timeline.

Recalculating the amortization schedule allows you to visualize how much interest you'll save over the life of the loan and how many years you've shaved off your mortgage.

There are various online tools, such as Karl's Mortgage Calculator, that can help you easily calculate the effects of lump-sum payments. These tools can also help you track your progress and make informed decisions about further payments.

For instance, using an amortization calculator, you can input the new mortgage balance of $150,000 and see how your future payments will be split between principal and interest. You'll likely notice that your monthly payment will remain the same, but the portion of the payment that goes toward the principal will increase, while the portion that goes toward interest will decrease. Over time, this strategy can drastically reduce the length of your mortgage and the overall amount of interest paid.

Recalculating your amortization schedule after each lump-sum payment gives you the ability to track the impact of your efforts and helps you stay motivated as you watch the principal balance decrease more quickly than it would under the traditional schedule.

Step 4: Track Your Progress

Consistency is key when it comes to making lump-sum payments toward your mortgage. As you continue to make additional payments toward the principal, you'll see your progress speed up significantly. Each time you apply a lump sum, you'll notice that more of your future payments are directed toward the principal, and less toward interest.

You can continue using the PLOC to make further lump-sum payments as you have the opportunity. If you receive a bonus, a tax refund, or a windfall of any kind, consider using those funds to pay down your mortgage. The more you reduce your principal balance, the faster you'll be able to eliminate your mortgage entirely.

This is where the true power of this strategy lies: by constantly reducing the balance, you're decreasing the overall interest burden. Over the years, this can result in substantial savings and a much quicker path to homeownership.

As you track your progress, be sure to keep a close eye on your overall financial situation. While using a PLOC to pay down your mortgage is an effective strategy, it's essential to ensure that you're not over-leveraging yourself. Always be mindful of your ability to repay the PLOC balance to avoid potential financial strain.

Transitioning to a HELOC for Further Mortgage Paydown

Now that you've reduced your mortgage balance using the PLOC strategy, you may find that you've hit a point where the available credit on your PLOC is nearing its limit, or you're looking for a more structured way to continue paying off your mortgage faster. This is where transitioning to a HELOC comes into play.

The HELOC offers several advantages over a PLOC, including lower interest rates, a revolving credit line, and higher borrowing limits based on your home equity. As your mortgage balance decreases, you can use the available equity in your home through a HELOC to continue paying down your mortgage more aggressively, potentially at a lower interest rate and with more flexible borrowing options.

Understanding your mortgage amortization schedule, along with how lump-sum payments can impact it, gives you a clear strategy for debt reduction. Transitioning to a HELOC after using a PLOC allows you to tap into even more powerful tools for accelerating your mortgage payoff and building wealth. In the next chapter, we'll explore how to leverage the HELOC's flexibility to make even larger payments toward your mortgage, ensuring a fast track to financial freedom.

Understanding the Amortization Schedule and Using a PLOC to Accelerate Your Payoff

An amortization schedule is a detailed table that shows how each payment on a loan is split into two parts: the interest and the principal. It helps borrowers understand how much they are paying for the loan itself and how much they are paying for the privilege of borrowing money. An amortization schedule is not just an administrative tool; it is central to managing and understanding your mortgage, as it reveals how your loan balance will reduce over time and how the interest is distributed throughout the loan's life.

Interest vs. Principal

When you first take out a mortgage, the balance on the loan is at its highest. During this time, the majority of your monthly payment is used to cover the interest, rather than reducing the principal. This is due to the way interest is calculated—on the remaining balance. Since the starting balance is large, the interest payments are also large. For example, if you have a mortgage of $300,000 at 4% interest, the interest in the first month alone could amount to several thousand dollars. As the balance decreases with each payment, the interest portion of your payments gradually shrinks, and more of your payment begins to reduce the principal.

In the early years, homeowners often feel as though they are not making significant progress in paying down the loan. This is because the interest on the large balance takes up much of the payment. For instance, in the first few years, you might find that only a small fraction of your monthly payment actually goes toward reducing the principal, even though you're making regular payments.

Early Payment Structure and Its Implications

The structure of mortgage payments can feel frustrating for many homeowners. The early payments are heavily weighted toward interest. For example, in a 30-year mortgage, the first several years could see only a small percentage of each payment going toward the principal. This early payment structure is what makes mortgage payoffs feel slow, and it contributes to the long timeline of paying off a traditional mortgage. Even though homeowners are making regular payments, the loan balance doesn't reduce as quickly as they might expect.

The concept of an amortization curve explains this. In the early years, the curve is steep, with a high proportion of payments going toward interest. Over time, as the balance decreases, the curve flattens, and the principal is reduced at a faster rate. Understanding this structure can help homeowners set expectations about how long it will take to pay off their loan and how much interest they will pay over time.

How a PLOC Helps Accelerate Payoff

A Personal Line of Credit (PLOC) can be a game-changer in accelerating mortgage payoff. It is essentially a revolving credit line, much like a credit card, that you can draw from to make lump-sum payments toward your mortgage principal. The idea is to reduce the principal more quickly than the regular payment schedule allows, resulting in significant interest savings and a faster path to mortgage freedom.

Reduce the Loan Balance Faster

One of the main advantages of using a PLOC is that it allows you to make lump-sum payments toward your mortgage principal. When you apply this strategy, you directly reduce the balance of your mortgage. Lowering the principal balance has a direct effect on the amount of interest you pay over the life of the loan because mortgage interest is calculated based on the outstanding balance. The more you reduce the balance, the less interest accrues on the remaining loan amount.

For example, if you have a mortgage balance of $250,000 and make a lump-sum payment of $50,000 from your PLOC, your mortgage balance is immediately reduced to $200,000. This reduction in balance means that subsequent monthly payments will incur less interest, saving you money over the long term.

Interest Savings

The real power of using a PLOC to pay down your mortgage lies in the interest savings. Mortgage interest is typically calculated monthly, based on the remaining balance. So, the more you reduce the balance early, the less interest will accrue, and the more of each future payment will go toward reducing the principal.

Over time, the amount of interest you save can be substantial. For example, if you make a $50,000 lump-sum payment from your PLOC, that could save you tens of thousands of dollars in interest over the life of a 30-year mortgage. This is because the loan balance is lower, so the amount of interest charged each month is reduced.

More of Your Payment Goes Toward the Principal

Once you reduce the mortgage balance with a lump-sum payment, more of your monthly payment will go toward reducing the principal. This is a key concept in amortization—as the principal balance decreases, the portion of your monthly payment that applies to the principal increases, while the interest portion decreases.

For example, after making the lump-sum payment, you'll notice that a larger percentage of your next monthly payment goes toward principal repayment, rather than interest. This compounding effect works in your favor: by reducing the balance early, you ensure that future payments are more effective at paying down the loan.

This shift accelerates the reduction of the principal, leading to faster mortgage payoff. The earlier you reduce the principal, the greater the compounding effect, which further speeds up the process. Essentially, the use of a PLOC can turn what is normally a slow and tedious mortgage payoff process into a faster, more efficient one.

Shifting the Amortization Curve

The traditional amortization curve can feel like a slow process. Early on, the curve is steep, with much of your monthly payment going toward interest. But when you make a lump-sum payment from your PLOC, you effectively shift this curve. The large reduction in the principal balance causes the balance to decline more rapidly, which means you'll pay off your loan much faster than the original schedule would suggest.

Instead of waiting 15 or 20 years for your mortgage to reduce significantly, making a lump-sum payment with a PLOC gives you a head start. The earlier in the mortgage term you make this payment, the greater the impact, because it shifts the amortization curve sooner and faster.

Using a Personal Line of Credit (PLOC) to pay down your mortgage is a powerful strategy for homeowners who want to accelerate their mortgage payoff and save on interest. By understanding how the amortization schedule works, you can take advantage of the compounding benefits that come with reducing your mortgage balance early on. The faster you reduce your principal, the less interest you will pay over the life of the loan, and the quicker you will own your home outright. With careful planning and strategic use of a PLOC, you can dramatically improve your financial situation, paying off your mortgage sooner and saving thousands of dollars in interest.

If you have a $200,000 mortgage with a 4% interest rate, the early years of the mortgage may see minimal principal reduction. However, by making a $50,000 lump-sum payment toward the principal using a PLOC, you can reduce your mortgage balance to $150,000. With the new balance, your interest payments will be lower, and more of each payment will go toward paying down the principal. This can save you thousands of dollars in interest over the life of the loan.

Year	Interest	Principal	Total	LTV	Balance
2000	7,935.89	3,522.07	11,457.97	98.2	196,477.93
2001	7,792.40	3,665.57	11,457.97	96.4	192,812.36
2002	7,643.06	3,814.91	11,457.97	94.5	188,997.45
2003	7,487.63	3,970.33	11,457.97	92.5	185,027.12
2004	7,325.88	4,132.09	11,457.97	90.4	180,895.03
2005	7,157.53	4,300.44	11,457.97	88.3	176,594.59
2006	6,982.32	4,475.65	11,457.97	86.1	172,118.94
2007	6,799.98	4,657.99	11,457.97	83.7	167,460.95
2008	6,610.20	4,847.76	11,457.97	81.3	162,613.19
2009	6,412.70	5,045.27	11,457.97	78.8	157,567.92
2010	6,207.15	5,250.82	11,457.97	76.2	152,317.10
2011	5,993.22	5,464.75	11,457.97	73.4	146,852.35
2012	5,770.58	5,687.39	11,457.97	70.6	141,164.96
2013	**5,538.86**	**5,919.10**	**11,457.97**	**67.6**	**135,245.86**
2014	5,297.71	6,160.26	11,457.97	64.5	129,085.60
2015	5,046.73	6,411.23	11,457.97	61.3	122,674.36
2016	4,785.53	6,672.44	11,457.97	58.0	116,001.93
2017	4,513.68	6,944.28	11,457.97	54.5	109,057.64
2018	4,230.76	7,227.20	11,457.97	50.9	101,830.44
2019	3,936.31	7,521.65	11,457.97	47.2	94,308.78
2020	3,629.87	7,828.10	11,457.97	43.2	86,480.69
2021	3,310.94	8,147.02	11,457.97	39.2	78,333.66
2022	2,979.02	8,478.95	11,457.97	34.9	69,854.72
2023	2,633.57	8,824.39	11,457.97	30.5	61,030.32
2024	2,274.06	9,183.91	11,457.97	25.9	51,846.41
2025	1,899.89	9,558.08	11,457.97	21.1	42,288.33
2026	1,510.48	9,947.49	11,457.97	16.2	32,340.84
2027	1,105.20	10,352.77	11,457.97	11.0	21,988.08
2028	683.41	10,774.55	11,457.97	5.6	11,213.53
2029	244.44	11,213.53	11,457.97	0.0	0.00

Understanding the Amortization Schedule and Using a PLOC to Accelerate Your Payoff

The amortization schedule is one of the most important tools in mortgage management, yet it often goes underappreciated. It shows you exactly how your payments are applied to the mortgage, separating them into two categories: interest and principal. Early in a mortgage, most of your payments go toward paying interest, and only a small portion goes toward reducing the actual loan balance. This is due to the fact that interest is calculated on the remaining balance of the loan, and when you first start making payments, the balance is at its highest.

Let's take a closer look at how this works, using a real-world example and the impact of a lump-sum payment toward your mortgage using a Personal Line of Credit (PLOC). By leveraging the power of offset banking and velocity banking, you can drastically reduce the time it takes to pay off your mortgage and cut down on the amount of interest you pay over the life of the loan.

The Real-World Example

Let's consider a $200,000 mortgage with a 4% interest rate, paid over a 30-year term. Based on a standard mortgage, you would expect to pay about $955 per month, with the interest portion of the payment taking up most of the early years. Over the first few years, a very small portion of your payment goes toward paying down the principal. As seen in the chart, during the first 12 years, your principal reduction is minimal compared to the amount of money you're paying in interest.

In fact, looking at the amortization schedule, it's not until 2013—after 12 years of payments—that the curve of the amortization schedule really starts to shift. During this time, you're paying large amounts of interest, and the portion of your payments that go toward reducing the principal is small.

The Amortization Curve: Before the Shift

When looking at an amortization schedule, the curve of interest and principal payments is steep at the beginning of the loan term. At the start, nearly all of your monthly payments are applied toward the interest on the loan, and only a small fraction goes toward reducing the principal. In the case of this mortgage, you're not really starting to make a significant dent in the loan balance until around 2013, when you've made about 12 years of payments.

This is the reality for many homeowners: the early years of a mortgage are mostly focused on paying interest, and it can feel like your payments aren't making much progress toward reducing your debt. In this scenario, it will take over 12 years of regular payments before you see a significant shift toward paying down your loan principal.

And here's where the impact of this interest becomes more apparent. If you were to only make the normal monthly payments over the 30-year term, you would end up paying a total of $143,739.01 in interest alone—which is nearly as much as the original loan amount itself.

This is where things get extreme. In today's world, with fluctuating interest rates and higher home prices, this burden is often even worse. The interest you pay over the course of a mortgage can be substantial, and this is why it's crucial to consider strategies like Velocity Banking to accelerate the payoff process and reduce the total amount of interest you pay.

How a Lump-Sum Payment Cuts Years Off Your Mortgage

Now, let's assume that instead of making the regular payments, you decide to use a PLOC to make a lump-sum payment towards your mortgage. In this example, let's say you use a $50,000 lump-sum payment from your PLOC. By doing this, you immediately reduce the principal balance of your mortgage from $200,000 to $150,000. This lump-sum payment has an immediate effect:

- The interest payments will be drastically reduced, because they are now based on a smaller balance.
- More of your monthly payments will now go toward the principal, since less of your payment is being absorbed by interest.

As a result, the curve of your amortization schedule shifts. Instead of the long, gradual reduction of principal that occurs over 12 years, you've essentially "jump-started" your mortgage payoff. With the balance reduced, you can start seeing your mortgage principal go down faster, cutting years off the term of the loan.

This reduction in principal also means that over the remaining life of the loan, you'll pay much less interest. The faster you pay down the loan, the less interest accrues on the outstanding balance, leading to substantial savings over time. In fact, this lump-sum payment could potentially cut several years off your mortgage, depending on the size of the payment and the remaining term.

Cutting Out Interest and Gaining Freedom

The financial benefit of making a lump-sum payment and using a PLOC in this manner is undeniable. When you reduce the principal early, you are also eliminating the high-interest payments that would have been eating up your monthly payment for years. This is the true magic of velocity banking—by paying off chunks of your debt early and using tools like a PLOC and offset banking, you can reduce both your mortgage term and the interest you'll end up paying.

Let's pause for a moment to reflect on the financial impact of this strategy. If you were to continue paying your mortgage with only the standard payments, you would pay $143,739.01 in interest over the full 30 years. However, by making a lump-sum payment and reducing your mortgage balance, you are directly cutting down on the interest you would otherwise be charged. Even if you make one lump-sum payment early in the loan term, this could save you tens of thousands of dollars in interest, while also accelerating your mortgage payoff.

For example, let's say that by using a lump-sum payment of $50,000, you cut five years off the term of your mortgage. This means that not only will you have your mortgage paid off five years earlier, but you will also have saved a significant amount of interest that you would have paid had you continued making regular payments for the full 30 years. The total savings can amount to tens of thousands of dollars, possibly even more, depending on how quickly you can pay down your mortgage.

This is especially important in today's economic climate, where mortgage interest rates are rising and home prices continue to climb. The longer you wait to pay off your mortgage, the more interest you will pay. By taking action now and reducing the principal as quickly as possible, you can save significantly on interest over the life of the loan.

Using Velocity Banking and Offset Banking for Financial Independence

Velocity banking isn't just about making lump-sum payments. It's a comprehensive strategy that uses offset banking as a tool to make payments faster. With offset banking, you can deposit your entire paycheck into the PLOC and use that balance to offset the mortgage balance.

The key here is that instead of letting the balance of your PLOC sit idle, you can offset the interest that accrues daily on your mortgage. By doing this, you significantly reduce the amount of interest that's charged, because the bank calculates interest on the average daily balance. This means that every time you deposit your paycheck into the PLOC, you reduce the average daily balance, which in turn reduces the interest charged.

Using this technique, you can pay off your mortgage faster, while keeping your overall cash flow intact. The key is to use the PLOC as a strategic financial tool to make your money work for you, reducing your mortgage balance, paying less interest, and putting you on the fast track to financial independence.

By paying down your mortgage with velocity banking, you're not just achieving a debt-free lifestyle—you're positioning yourself for financial growth. The sooner you eliminate your mortgage, the sooner you can use the funds that would have gone toward interest payments to invest in your future. Whether that's investing in real estate, stocks, or other income-generating investments, being free of your mortgage allows you to put your money to work for you— helping you build wealth and create the financial freedom you desire.

The Path to Financial Freedom

By leveraging the amortization schedule and understanding how lump-sum payments, PLOCs, and velocity banking work together, you can make your mortgage payoff much faster and more efficient. The key insight is that you don't have to wait 12 years before the principal starts significantly reducing—by applying lump-sum payments early in the loan, you can shorten the mortgage term and save thousands of dollars in interest payments.

Not only does this make your home ownership more affordable in the long run, but it gives you the opportunity to invest in your future, building assets that will help you achieve financial freedom.

Using velocity banking and offset banking is a game-changer. By utilizing these strategies to reduce debt faster, you gain access to greater financial flexibility, more control over your finances, and a clear path toward investing and growing your wealth.

This approach to mortgage payoff doesn't just make you debt-free sooner—it creates the freedom to invest, build, and live life without the weight of long-term debt hanging over your head.

PUTTING IT ALL TOGETHER

As we draw toward the conclusion of this guide, it's important to take a step back and recognize that all the strategies, techniques, and financial concepts explored throughout the book are just part of a larger journey. The real key to financial success lies not only in applying these strategies effectively but also in cultivating the right mindset and behaviors that will support and sustain long-term success. In this chapter, we'll integrate everything we've discussed so far and offer guidance on how to move forward on your journey to financial freedom.

The Power of Mindset in Financial Success

Mindset is often the unsung hero when it comes to achieving financial freedom. You can be armed with the most sophisticated strategies, a well-structured plan, and even a significant income, but if your mindset is not aligned with your financial goals, your progress will likely be slow, or you might even derail your efforts. Financial success is built on the foundation of a resilient mindset that shapes how you approach money, make decisions, and deal with the challenges that inevitably arise.

At the heart of a strong financial mindset is the ability to practice delayed gratification. In today's fast-paced world, the temptation of instant rewards is everywhere. Whether it's purchasing the latest gadgets, eating out at expensive restaurants, or indulging in other short-term pleasures, the pull of immediate satisfaction can be powerful. However, achieving financial freedom requires you to put these temporary pleasures aside in favor of long-term goals. It's about making sacrifices today to enjoy the fruits of your labor tomorrow.

Delayed gratification means that you recognize the importance of investing in your future by saving, budgeting, and making wise financial decisions now. It involves consciously choosing to forgo spending today in favor of building a solid financial foundation that will support you in the years to come. Those who master delayed gratification are more likely to enjoy lasting wealth and financial freedom.

Furthermore, self-discipline is the backbone of the entire financial journey. Without the ability to stick to a budget, avoid emotional spending, and stay committed to long-term goals, it's easy to fall into bad habits. Consistent action, even when it feels difficult or inconvenient, is what will ultimately lead to success. Financial independence isn't about perfection—it's about remaining focused, even when things aren't going perfectly.

A growth mindset is also essential for building wealth. Individuals with a growth mindset believe that their financial success can improve through effort, learning, and persistence. Rather than viewing obstacles as insurmountable roadblocks, they see them as opportunities to learn and grow. By adopting this mindset, you can push through challenges, adapt your strategies as needed, and keep progressing toward your goals. This mindset encourages continuous education, growth, and a deeper understanding of personal finance, ensuring that you never stop striving to improve.

Finally, we must acknowledge that financial setbacks are inevitable. Whether due to a market downturn, an unexpected expense, or a temporary income loss, challenges are an unavoidable part of the process. However, the true measure of success lies in how you respond to these setbacks. Are you able to bounce back quickly? Can you learn from these situations and adjust your approach? The ability to recover and adapt is a defining trait of those who ultimately achieve financial freedom.

The Debt-Free Life and What Comes Next

Achieving a debt-free life is one of the most significant milestones on your journey to financial independence. There's a profound sense of relief and freedom that comes with eliminating the weight of debt. Once you pay off your debt, it's like lifting a heavy burden off your shoulders. But the benefits of debt elimination go far beyond just feeling financially lighter. When you are no longer weighed down by debt payments, your cash flow improves, and you have more financial resources to invest and grow your wealth.

Paying off your debt means that you are no longer committed to monthly interest payments. As a result, the money you were previously using to service debt is freed up to be used for more productive purposes. You can now invest in stocks, real estate, or even start your own business—options that would have been unavailable to you while you were still tied to debt obligations. This newfound financial flexibility is what makes a debt-free life so empowering.

With your finances in a more stable position, you are also able to refocus your mindset. No longer bogged down by liabilities, you are free to pursue your financial goals with renewed clarity and confidence. You can now take a long-term view of your wealth-building efforts. The feeling of liberation is not just about eliminating financial pressure; it's about gaining the freedom to direct your money where it will benefit you most.

Additionally, financial freedom opens up opportunities for personal growth and more meaningful life experiences. You can spend more time with your loved ones, travel the world, or pursue new passions. The possibilities are endless when you are no longer bogged down by debt. When your money is no longer tied up in interest payments, you can focus on building a life that aligns with your values, passions, and personal desires.

Moreover, living debt-free gives you peace of mind. The constant worry about interest rates, loan balances, and minimum payments disappears, allowing you to focus on what truly matters to you. Your mental and emotional well-being improve as you gain control over your finances and remove the stress that debt can impose.

Building a Financial Freedom Plan

Achieving financial freedom is not something that happens by accident. It requires a well-crafted plan, discipline, and consistent effort. Transitioning from debt-heavy living to financial independence demands a structured, step-by-step approach. Here's a comprehensive framework for creating your financial freedom plan:

1. Set Clear Goals: The first and most crucial step in your financial journey is to set clear, measurable

goals. Financial freedom means different things to different people, so it's essential to define what it looks like for you. For some, it might involve becoming completely debt-free and building an emergency savings fund. For others, it could mean acquiring a portfolio of rental properties or starting a business. The key is to be specific about what you want and break down those goals into achievable steps. The more defined your goals are, the easier it will be to align your actions with them.

2. Start with the Basics: Once your goals are in place, start with the basics. Your first priority should be eliminating high-interest debt, such as credit card balances, personal loans, and car loans. Velocity Banking is an excellent strategy to help you pay off debt more quickly by leveraging a Home Equity Line of Credit (HELOC) or a Personal Line of Credit (PLOC). By consolidating high-interest debt into lower-interest options, you can pay off your balance faster and more efficiently. Once you are debt-free, you will have more disposable income to invest and grow your wealth.

3. Create a Budget: A solid budget is the foundation of financial success. Creating a budget allows you to track your income and expenses, ensuring that your money is being allocated to your most important financial priorities. A budget helps prevent unnecessary spending and makes sure that you are saving and investing enough to meet your goals. It's an ongoing process, so be sure to review and adjust your budget regularly to keep it aligned with your financial situation.

4. Commit to Consistency: Financial success is a marathon, not a sprint. Consistency is key to

building wealth and achieving your goals. You will face obstacles along the way, and there will be times when it feels like your progress is slow. But the key is to stay focused and committed to your plan, even during difficult times. Every step you take, no matter how small, is helping you build momentum toward financial independence.
5. Review and Adjust: As you move forward on your financial journey, it's essential to periodically review your progress. Are you on track to meet your debt reduction targets? Are your investments performing as expected? Regularly evaluating your plan helps you identify areas where improvements can be made. If something isn't working, make adjustments. Financial planning is dynamic, and your strategy should evolve as your situation changes.

The Bigger Picture—Financial Freedom Beyond Debt Elimination

While eliminating debt is an essential part of the journey, financial freedom is about more than just becoming debt-free. The true goal of financial freedom is to build wealth, expand your assets, and create a life where you have the flexibility to make decisions based on your values, not your financial obligations.

Once you've eliminated your debt and freed up more of your cash flow, it's time to focus on wealth accumulation. The first step is to invest—whether in stocks, real estate, or even your own business. Investments can generate passive income, which can be reinvested to acquire more assets. This cycle of reinvestment and growth can allow you to build significant wealth over time.

Additionally, financial freedom provides the flexibility to explore new opportunities. Whether that means traveling, spending more time with family, or pursuing a passion project, financial independence gives you the freedom to direct your time, energy, and resources toward what matters most to you.

Financial freedom also gives you the ability to create a legacy. You can pass down wealth and financial wisdom to future generations, ensuring that your financial success endures beyond your lifetime. Whether it's through charitable contributions, investments, or setting up a family trust, you can make a lasting impact on the lives of others.

STEP-BY-STEP GUIDE TO USING VELOCITY AND OFFSET BANKING TOGETHER

Step 1: Obtain a Personal Line of Credit (PLOC)

The first step is to secure a Personal Line of Credit (PLOC) or a Home Equity Line of Credit (HELOC). You'll use this line of credit as your main tool to reduce debt and manage cash flow.

- Where to get a PLOC:
    - Banks: Contact your bank or credit union where you have an existing account. Start by asking for a PLOC and inquire about interest rates, terms, and fees. Some banks offer special rates for existing customers, so it's worth exploring those.
    - Online Lenders: Online lending platforms also offer PLOCs with competitive rates. Research and compare various online lenders to find one that fits your needs.
    - Home Equity Line of Credit (HELOC): If you have equity in your home, consider applying

for a HELOC. This option typically offers lower interest rates compared to unsecured PLOCs.
- How to apply: Gather your financial documents, such as proof of income, credit report, and debt-to-income ratio, as lenders will assess these to determine your eligibility.

Step 2: Use Your PLOC as Your Primary Account

Once you have access to a PLOC, make it your primary account by having all your income deposited into it.

- How to set this up:
  - Change the direct deposit settings with your employer so your paycheck goes directly into your PLOC.
  - If you receive income through other means (e.g., freelance work, side gigs), ensure these payments also go into your PLOC.
- Why this works:
  - By depositing your income directly into your PLOC, you increase the balance temporarily, but this also reduces the amount of interest you pay on the overall balance.
  - The interest you pay on a PLOC is calculated daily, so depositing income quickly reduces the average daily balance, which minimizes interest.

Step 3: Pay Down High-Interest Debt with Your PLOC

Now that your income is flowing into your PLOC, it's time to use the available balance to pay off high-interest debt.

- Paying down debt:
  - List all of your current high-interest debts (credit cards, personal loans, etc.).
  - Determine which debt has the highest interest rate, and use the PLOC to pay it off

first. This can be done in full or through partial payments to reduce the balance.
- Why this works:
  - By transferring high-interest debt to the PLOC, you significantly reduce the amount of interest you'll pay over time, as PLOCs typically have lower interest rates than credit cards and personal loans.
- Important note: Ensure that you make minimum payments on other debts to avoid late fees or penalties while you focus on paying them off with the PLOC.

Step 4: Withdraw for Expenses and Payments

After using the PLOC to pay off high-interest debt, the next step is to use it for day-to-day living expenses.

- How to withdraw for expenses:
  - Use your PLOC to cover monthly bills (utilities, rent, car payments, groceries, etc.). You can either make direct payments from the PLOC or transfer the funds to your regular checking account to pay these expenses.
  - Keep track of your expenses to ensure that you aren't withdrawing more than necessary. Withdrawals should be made only for necessary expenses or as a part of your financial plan.
- Why this works:
  - By using the PLOC for everyday expenses, you ensure that your money is minimizing interest. Since the balance of your PLOC temporarily increases, it's important to deposit your income quickly after each withdrawal to reduce the balance as soon

as possible.

Step 5: Deposit Income Back Into Your PLOC as Quickly as Possible

The key to minimizing interest payments is to keep your PLOC balance as low as possible. After withdrawing funds for expenses, deposit your income back into the PLOC immediately.

- Why this matters:
  - The faster you deposit income, the sooner the interest on your PLOC is minimized. Because interest on a PLOC is calculated daily, a high balance left for an extended period will accumulate more interest. By depositing income immediately after withdrawals, you reduce the balance and keep interest charges low.
- How to do this:
  - Ensure that any extra payments you make towards your debts or other expenses are also deposited back into your PLOC immediately.
  - Track your income and withdrawals to maintain a disciplined flow of cash through the account.

Step 6: Continue the Cycle of Velocity and Offset Banking

The final step is to repeat this cycle consistently. By continuously using the PLOC to pay off debts, banking your income into the PLOC, and withdrawing for expenses, you are constantly reducing your interest payments, improving your cash flow, and accelerating debt repayment.

- Maintain the system:
  - Consistency is key. The more regularly you follow this cycle, the more money you'll save on interest, and the faster you'll pay

down debt.
- o Regularly monitor your cash flow and ensure you're staying on track with your budget and goals.
- Why this is effective:
  - o By combining Velocity Banking (paying down high-interest debt with the PLOC) and Offset Banking (minimizing interest on debts by depositing income into the PLOC), you create a financial ecosystem that reduces the interest you pay, increases your available cash flow, and accelerates your journey to debt freedom.

Note: Transition to Acquiring Assets Once Debt is Paid Off

Once all high-interest debt has been paid off and your PLOC balance is under control, this is the time to start acquiring assets.

- What to do next:
  - o With your debt eliminated, you can now focus on investing in assets that generate passive income, such as real estate, stocks, bonds, or business ventures.
  - o Use the additional cash flow you've freed up by reducing debt to fuel your asset-building strategy. This might include purchasing rental properties, investing in dividend stocks, or starting a side business.
- Why this matters:
  - o Acquiring assets, rather than continuing to pay off liabilities, allows you to build wealth and create long-term financial security. This shift in focus is the final stage of your financial journey, where you transition from managing debt to growing your wealth.

Final Tips for Success
1. Stay disciplined: Using this strategy effectively requires a high level of discipline. Keep track of all expenses and income, and stick to your plan to avoid unnecessary debt.
2. Avoid over-withdrawing: Only withdraw what's necessary to cover living expenses. Over-withdrawing from your PLOC will lead to a higher balance and more interest charges.
3. Review regularly: Periodically review your PLOC terms, interest rates, and your overall debt progress to ensure you are staying on track. Adjust your strategy as needed.
4. Build an emergency fund: While using a PLOC helps with cash flow, it's essential to have an emergency fund to cover unexpected expenses without relying too heavily on your PLOC.

ABOUT THE AUTHOR

B.F. Weaver is a passionate writer, entrepreneur, and devoted family man. With a deep commitment to achieving financial freedom, B.F. writes not only to share his knowledge but to inspire others on their own journey toward independence and success.

He is driven by the belief that true financial security can transform not only an individual's life but also the lives of those they love. When he's not writing, B.F spends his time with his wife and two daughters, always striving to build a brighter future for his family.

Through this book, B.F.] hopes to offer readers the tools and inspiration to break free from financial limitations and create lasting freedom for themselves and their loved ones.